CAREERS IN COMPUTER TECHNOLOGY™

CAREERS IN
Database
Design

ERIN K. MCGUIRE

ROSEN
PUBLISHING
NEW YORK

For my loves, Rowan and Malachi, you make my world go round. Deepest appreciation to Dean Maurice and Fred Leskowitz for sharing your knowledge and expertise.

Published in 2011 by The Rosen Publishing Group, Inc.
29 East 21st Street, New York, NY 10010

Copyright © 2011 by The Rosen Publishing Group, Inc.

First Edition

All rights reserved. No part of this book may be reproduced in any form without permission in writing from the publisher, except by a reviewer.

Library of Congress Cataloging-in-Publication Data

McGuire, Erin K.
 Careers in database design / Erin K. McGuire. — 1st ed.
     p. cm. — (Careers in computer technology)
 Includes bibliographical references and index.
 ISBN 978-1-4488-1317-9 (library binding)
 1. Database design—Vocational guidance—Juvenile literature. 2. Computer programming—Vocational guidance—Juvenile literature. I. Title.
 QA76.9.D26M43 2011
 004.023—dc22

                                                                    2010012660

Manufactured in the United States of America

CPSIA Compliance Information: Batch #W11YA: For further information, contact Rosen Publishing, New York, New York, at 1-800-237-9932.

On the cover: Database designers put the world of information into order.

Contents

Introduction 4

Chapter 1 Introduction to Database Design 6
Chapter 2 The Person Behind the Title 13
Chapter 3 Everything in Its Place: Organizing Data 23
Chapter 4 Managing Storage and Maintenance 34
Chapter 5 Avenues for Entering the Field 42
Chapter 6 An Array of Opportunities 52
Chapter 7 The Evolution of a Database Designer 60

Glossary 69
For More Information 71
For Further Reading 74
Bibliography 76
Index 78

INTRODUCTION

Imagine a warehouse full of files, the information within the files having no relationship to other information nearby, no rhyme or reason for its placement. How easy would it be to access information from that warehouse? It would be like finding a needle in a haystack! Now imagine the files are arranged according to their subjects. The files are in alphabetical order, and each file can be cross-referenced with other files. The task of pulling out any one piece of information is not so daunting if the information is organized in a manageable, predictable format.

A database is a digital warehouse. It can store a huge quantity of data, or information. In fact, there is no limit to the type of data that may be stored electronically. Within a computer database, businesses might keep product inventories, sales transactions, customer profiles, employee records, and financial records. Libraries, museums, research institutions, and government agencies store an enormous amount of data and may share this information with the public. The data may take the form of text, numerical figures, or even pictures, music, or videos. Input this information into a computer without a system for organizing it, and retrieving the data becomes something akin to finding that needle in the haystack.

Simply defined, the job of a database designer is to create a system for storing information within a database, allowing the data to be easily retrieved and updated. A person who has an eye for detail and can organize information in a logical fashion will receive great satisfaction from designing a database. This is a fast-paced, challenging career of the future.

Data storage has come a long way since the first personal computers came into use and disks were used for storage. Due to advances in technology, there are now many more electronic devices through which information can be accessed. The speed of information access is ever increasing. These rapid changes have had a positive impact on the field, as database designers have a huge market in which to offer their services. The decreasing cost of computer hardware has enabled many companies to invest resources in information storage and management. Many companies have increased the number of information technology professionals, including database designers, on staff.

In the Information Age, when there is so much data to be stored and organized, database designers are in high demand. Almost everyone uses the work of a database designer in some form at work and in daily life. As with any career, an understanding of the profession is key in developing a career path that allows one to grow and prosper. This book will help provide an understanding of the ever-changing field of database design.

CHAPTER 1

Introduction to Database Design

In the modern world, anyone who works with a computer likely uses a database on a regular basis. Individuals, businesses, and government agencies all use databases to store and look up information. A database designer's work often places him or her in the area of information technology (IT) within the computer field. However, databases are so widely used that there are opportunities for database designers to explore other areas of computer technology. Also, the information managed within databases covers a wide range of subject matter. This opens up the possibility for exposure to other interests and even hobbies while on the job.

WHAT IS A DATABASE?

A database is a collection of information. Information storage can take different forms. For example, when organizing information that is on paper, people often use a system of labeled folders that are stored alphabetically in filing cabinets. Electronic information storage has largely replaced these more archaic forms of storage. In the newer form of storage, the information is in a digital format that is accessible by computer or another electronic device. Electronic storage allows people to save much more information than they can physically house and access what they need quickly, often in just seconds.

INTRODUCTION TO DATABASE DESIGN | 7

Using a software program, data is entered into the computer. Later, a user can retrieve the information.

A database is put into electronic form by means of a software system called a database management system (DBMS). This software system is used to create the database and manage the information that is stored within it. Once information is saved in the database, it is not seen until a user poses a question to the system. Known as a query, the user's question enables the data to be pulled up on the screen. A database designer works with the DBMS, setting up a database that meets the organizational needs of the user and the requirements of the software system.

WHAT IS DATABASE DESIGN?

Database design is the process of taking information and organizing it into a manageable collection of material that users can access easily.

The design process has different parts or stages. For example, a database designer identifies users' needs, creates a database that will work well for the users, and then tests the system. After the database is set up, the designer makes sure that it continues to work properly. The designer often helps to solve any problems that arise and may help to change or expand the system. Making sure that the data is secure and adequately backed up is also extremely important. Therefore, database designers typically plan and test security measures as part of any database project.

Early in the design process, the database designer must consider how the user will search for information. For example, someone searching a database for a book about computer software can query the database. All of the books within the database that are related to the subject should come up. If the information is not properly organized or connected within the system, some data may be irretrievable.

Before putting information into a software system, the database designer makes a hard copy of the database structure. This hard copy is called a data model. There are many types of data models. Depending on the type of model used, the database structure may look like a diagram or chart when illustrated on paper. By using a database model, the designer can organize the information into categories and ensure that related material will be linked within the database.

WELL-DESIGNED DATABASES SUPPORT BUSINESS GROWTH

Imagine this scenario: a designer creates a database for a small online business. The database is designed to keep track of clients and orders. The business quickly becomes a huge success and orders begin to roll in. Luckily, the database designer considered the business's potential for rapid growth. The designer is able to quickly work changes into the database without downtime. What if the site had to shut down in order for the database to be revamped? The business would likely lose clients, as well as a lot of money, during the reconstruction of the database.

Because a database relies on a software system to run, a database designer must be comfortable working with different software applications. This helps the designer know what system would be a good fit for a particular database. Software designers and database designers often work in close company to the benefit of both professions.

BY ANY OTHER NAME

For the purposes of this book, the title database designer will be used to describe someone who organizes and maintains the storage of data. But other job titles may also be used and can be interchangeable. In some cases, however, there are differences in the emphasis of the job.

Database designers are sometimes referred to as database architects or database developers. These names stem from the use of a database model as a blueprint for the construction of the database. The titles database manager and database administrator are also used to describe positions related to databases. These titles can refer to everything from managing the design process to handling database security—and all that falls in between. Responsibilities may include verifying data integrity, troubleshooting, and disaster recovery.

One's job title may also depend on the size of the company for which one works or whether a worker is self-employed or not. When working for a big company that has a large IT team, one may have the opportunity to specialize in a particular aspect of information technology. On the other hand, someone who is self-employed or who works for a small company will probably have to wear many different hats, rather than having one area of expertise.

Database security and database performance tuning are two specialty areas within larger IT teams. With so much information accessible to so many, the field of database security has evolved out of necessity to help protect private and sensitive information. Positions as database security managers are common in financial institutions, for example. Performance tuning is an area in which one focuses on the running of the database. Someone in this role is not necessarily involved in designing the database. Professionals who do performance tuning ensure that the database is running efficiently. They also engage in problem solving to make it more efficient.

INTRODUCTION TO DATABASE DESIGN | 11

Portable electronic devices, such as this iPad, give database designers another outlet for their work and add to the growing demand for these professionals.

A WORLD OF OPTIONS

Computer professionals with knowledge of database design have many job options. For example, since a large amount of information is accessed through the World Wide Web, database designers may choose to work as, or with, Web page designers. Work requirements might include designing a database that can pull up information about a business, organize orders and sales, and keep data secure.

As portable electronic devices become more popular and advanced, people are able to access information on the go. As a result, a database designer might work in the field of computer engineering, developing software and hardware that enables information to be obtained on different devices. With new developments always occurring in the computer field, database designers will continually find new areas in which their expertise is required.

CHAPTER 2

The Person Behind the Title

Who are the multitalented people who put data in order, making life a little easier for those who need access to information? These professionals are people who possess the personal traits and professional skills to bring a design project to fruition.

PERSONAL QUALITIES

One's personal qualities or traits often make him or her more suitable for certain professions. Some employers place as much value on these personal attributes as they do education and experience. These characteristics are an asset to anyone in the computer field, including database designers.

At first glance, it may seem as if this profession is a solo act. However, depending on the work environment, interaction with others may be a routine part of the workday. For example, many database professionals work on an IT team, cooperating closely with software engineers, network administrators, computer programmers, or systems administrators to complete projects. The ability to communicate with others on the team, verbally and in writing, influences how successful the team is as a whole.

Strong communication skills also serve the database designer in relaying information about the function of the database to those not familiar with computer language. In many cases, a database is constructed for people outside of

Database designers are proficient at explaining the details of a design to others on the IT team, as well as to people who are unfamiliar with computer terminology.

the IT department, who may know little about how a database actually works. It then becomes the job of the designer to instruct the users on how to actually use the database. The database designer may develop and lead training sessions, which can take place one-on-one or in larger groups. If the database designer works at a help desk, interaction with users is a core requirement.

Written communication skills are helpful if the job entails writing out instructions on using the database. Again, being able to explain technical ideas in everyday language is important, since the users may have little to no knowledge of computer language. Some jobs also require written proposals or documentation. Documenting why the database was designed as it was can help the end user, enhancing the ease of access to information. Also, documentation can be helpful to the database designer in retracing steps in the design process should a problem come up.

In this field of systematizing information, logical thinking and attention to detail are necessities. The database designer must be able to analyze information and say, "This is how it should be organized." Numerous details, and all the possibilities for the retrieval of the information, must be considered when solving the problem of how to store the data. Lack of attention to something that may seem insignificant can be costly to a business. Larger errors even have the possibility of causing financial ruin if the database fails.

Computer technology is fast paced, and one must be adaptable in order to stay current in this field. Computer platforms and software that were standard last month may not be what is in use next month. Working in a field in which progress occurs at such a rapid pace can be exciting. The challenge is in keeping up with the new technology. What does this mean for the database designer? It means that the designer should have a thirst for learning, for increasing his or her own mental warehouse of information. A database designer should be able to change with the times in order to ensure a successful career.

PROFESSIONAL SKILLS

Once on the job, one's personal qualities will serve one well and complement the professional skills that come with experience. Certain professional skills are particularly important in the field of database design. For example, at first it may be a challenge to complete a project within a limited time frame. Developing good time management skills will increase productivity and benefit both the designer and the client. Often, a business or organization relies on the rapid development of an organizational system to be able to complete other tasks. If the design is not completed in a timely manner, it can cause everything else to run behind schedule. Good time management means determining what is a priority and then deciding in what order tasks should be completed.

Along with managing one's time, a database designer is required to make quick decisions that will determine

Time is of the essence when a database designer faces a project deadline.

the outcome of a project. Of course, decision-making skills develop over time as one becomes more confident in his or her abilities. However, doing research can go a long way in helping one make good decisions. In order to make decisions that are based on accurate information, the designer may need to research technical requirements, the history of a particular business, or future trends within a certain market.

Another beneficial skill that can develop with experience is juggling multiple tasks. Database designers often find themselves working on more than one project at a time or handling multiple aspects of a project. For example, a database designer may be fielding questions and learning about a new software system, even while designing a database.

While work is often divided among the whole IT team, database designers are often required to act independently. This is where all of these professional skills (time management, decision making, and multitasking) will serve the database designer well.

THE LIFE OF A DESIGN PROJECT

A database designer is assigned a design project; now where does he or she go from there? Before beginning the actual design, it is important for the database designer to have a clear understanding of the purpose of the database and the client's needs.

First, any information from the project is thoroughly reviewed so that the designer has a firm grasp of what the project entails and his or her role in completing it. With this understanding, the database designer might then develop a series of questions to ask the client in order to fill in his or

Members of the IT team gather information and exchange ideas to determine the best course of design development.

her knowledge about the needs of the end user. If the client knows little about information technology, the database designer may need to assist the client in determining exactly what the organization requires from the database.

Once these questions are answered, the database designer begins to analyze the information that will eventually be entered into the database. Through this process, the best means of organization, the type of data model, and the queries one can pose to the system are determined. The software application that will be used to house the database and manipulate the data is also considered. Throughout this phase of the project, the database designer may work closely with others on the IT team, such as software developers or project managers.

Next, the organization of information is given a concrete form by way of a data model. This is where the actual designing occurs and problem solving takes place. The designer tries to anticipate problems that could occur so as to prevent kinks in the system. He or she also creates problem-solving scenarios in case something goes awry once the system is up and running. The database designer keeps records of the design process and develops a backup and recovery plan. In this way, problems can be avoided entirely or, at the very least, quickly remedied.

Finally, the data is transferred to the software application that will support the database. This software allows the data to be input by manual typing. Then the data can be manipulated and managed within the system. Typically, a specialized computer language, called a query language, is used to access and change information within the database. Once the database is housed within an electronic device, the database designer monitors its performance. If there are flaws in the design, the designer may need to backtrack. This can increase the cost of the project and waste valuable time. If the database designer has been conscientious, the system will probably run smoothly.

The database designer gives the user instructions, in writing or verbally, about how to use the database. The instructions include the best ways to query the database in order to pull information. Now the design is complete, the database is up and running, and it is put into the hands of the user. At this point, a database designer may still play an important role in supporting the functioning of the database. The designer

ASKING THE RIGHT QUESTIONS

The following are questions for a database designer to consider when working on a design project:

1. What purpose will the database serve?
2. What is the budget for this project, and how can the design support cost-effectiveness?
3. What software application would best support the database?
4. What queries would allow information to be quickly and accurately retrieved from the database?
5. How should information be organized in order to maintain the integrity of the data (the completeness and accuracy of the information), even as data is changed?
6. In what way might the design need to evolve as the needs of the user change—through business growth, for example?
7. What problems may occur, and how can the system be backed up?
8. Is it necessary to provide a security system for the database?

may be required to run queries when needed or may stay on the project to help maintain the database as additions and other changes are made.

If something goes wrong with the database, the designer will be the first one contacted because he or she knows the details of the system. This is when the records made during the design process may be revisited and the backup and recovery plan put into effect. Depending on the position and the work environment, a database designer may be on call twenty-four hours a day, seven days a week, to repair a failing system.

Due to the amount of change in this field, some designers work mainly on upgrading databases. This involves taking a database, which one may or may not have designed, and updating the software or the database design so that it can run more efficiently.

PROFILE OF A PROFESSIONAL

Fred Leskowitz is a designer who is willing to change with the times. He is currently working with Thomson Reuters, a company that serves as an information resource for businesses and professionals. Leskowitz's career began twenty-five years ago, when he did an internship while studying library science. Leskowitz explains, "My first internship at library school consisted of sorting boxes—many, many boxes—of patent documents prior to being data-entered. By understanding the collection of data firsthand, I had many ideas about how to design the database that turned out to be quite useful in my next internship and job."

After receiving a bachelor of arts degree in aesthetics and technology and a masters degree in library science, Leskowitz went on to work in the field of library science. "Mainly I worked on library-related applications like card catalogs, collections, and inventory," he says. He then began working with a Thomson Reuters business called Micropatent. "I am often pulling information from other business systems to store and analyze," says Leskowitz. He gives an overview of a recent project: "[I] built a reporting screen window for customer service to pull usage reports by customer/date/product."

In combining his own interests with his work in database design, Leskowitz gains new perspective and keeps his work interesting. He explains, "My interest was in library science, specifically patents and trademarks. Though I now only deal with the accounting side of the products we sell because it is related to that field, there is always something interesting to consider. How many patents were sold in the field of library science, or related to music, my hobby? To answer those questions is simple, but having some touchstone into my own interest may provide additional insight into how to answer them."

His suggestion for prospective database designers is: "Choose to work in an industry or specialty that has interest to you—if you're interested in cars, then look for a database design position in the auto industry. The tools and techniques of database design are the same, but you'll be dealing with a subject area that has personal interest."

Database professionals use a combination of personal qualities, professional skills, an understanding of the job at hand, and sometimes even their own interests to complete a project. As long as one's qualities and interests match the general profile of a database designer, many of the specific job-related skills can be learned.

CHAPTER 3

Everything in Its Place: Organizing Data

The main objective of a database designer is to organize information. To accomplish this, the designer uses certain tools. These tools allow the designer to find a logical place for the information to be stored, while at the same time enabling the information to be retrieved easily. As with any cleanup job, it makes sense to put related information in the same place. For example, when organizing a house, a toothbrush would not be placed with the silverware. Finding connections within the data makes the information in the database more accessible to the end user.

DATABASE TERMINOLOGY

It does not take long to recognize that database design has a vocabulary all its own. Learning the technical terms that are used in the profession will help one to understand the functioning of a database and the job of a designer. Many of the terms are universally used in the design field. The following information gives an idea of the general database setup. However, the vocabulary can be different depending on the database system or model.

A number of important terms come into play as the database designer creates the data model. The database is the computer's warehouse of related information, or data. The

DBMS is a collection of computer programs, which are also referred to as software applications. These play a role in the development and management of the database. A database can be set up in a computer with the installation of software. Data entry is the means of putting new information into the database.

On the other side is the retrieval of data. A query is a question that is entered into the database in order to extract information. An example of a query is typing a question into a World Wide Web search engine and then having the data displayed on the screen. The designer must identify and set up the best ways for users to query the database in order to

Data is input into the software system using computer language or coding. Posing a query to the system enables the information to be retrieved.

EVERYTHING IN ITS PLACE: ORGANIZING DATA | 25

get quick and accurate results. Without effective ways to query the database, the data may be inaccessible and the database becomes obsolete.

The database designer also sets up the user interface for the database. The user interface is the point of communication between the user and the computer. Typically, a person first makes a connection to the database visually. He or she sees the information on a screen, such as a computer screen, mobile phone, or other electronic device. The person also interacts with the database through the user interface. In addition to typing in text boxes, the user may be able to use tools such as pull-down menus or checkboxes. The database

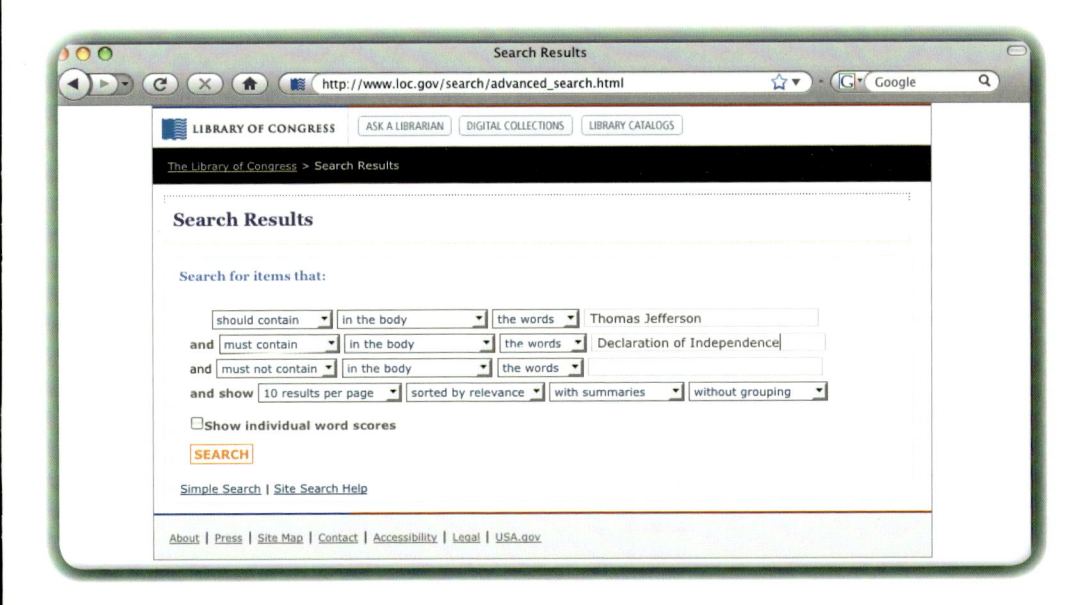

The screen is the user interface, or the place where the user can interact with the data stored within the database.

designer's goal is to set up the user interface so that the users can find what they need quickly and easily.

Database designers use structured query language (SQL), a programming language, to enter and manipulate data within the database. Knowledge of SQL is a must for designers, as it is used with the relational database, the most common type of database model.

A relational database contains a number of different elements. The structure of the database contains one or more tables. These tables are called relations because they consist of related information in a chartlike form. As an example, consider a database that houses information about bands. One table within the database may list information about rock bands, while another may list information about jazz bands.

Within each table, there are records and fields. Each record includes all of the information about a particular member of the table. In the example of rock bands, one record would include all of the information about a single rock band, like U2. Each field provides a particular piece of information about the bands in the table, like the names of band members, or the names of the band's CDs.

DATABASE MODEL TO DATABASE: A BLUEPRINT

A database is a big expense. It can become an even bigger expense if it does not function properly. The database designer works out as many kinks as possible on paper beforehand. This hard copy version of the database is called a database model. The model serves as a blueprint for how the data will

EVERYTHING IN ITS PLACE: ORGANIZING DATA | 27

Conceptual Data Model for Musicians in a Band
Source: DatabaseAnswers.org
(http://www.databaseanswers.org)

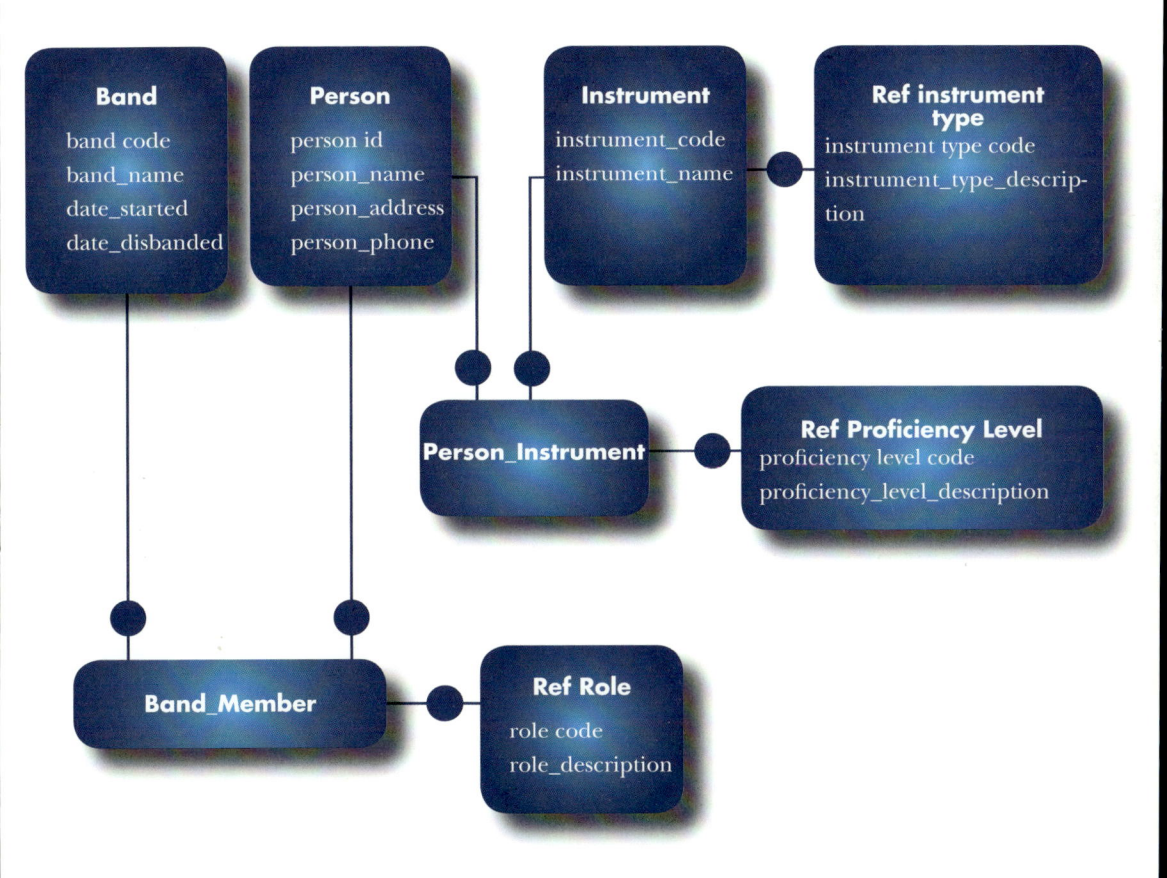

Band
band code
band_name
date_started
date_disbanded

Person
person id
person_name
person_address
person_phone

Instrument
instrument_code
instrument_name

Ref instrument type
instrument type code
instrument_type_description

Person_Instrument

Ref Proficiency Level
proficiency level code
proficiency_level_description

Band_Member

Ref Role
role code
role_description

A functional database is based on a well-planned database model.

28 | CAREERS IN DATABASE DESIGN

Creating a database model can involve trial and error before the designer finds the right structure for organizing the data.

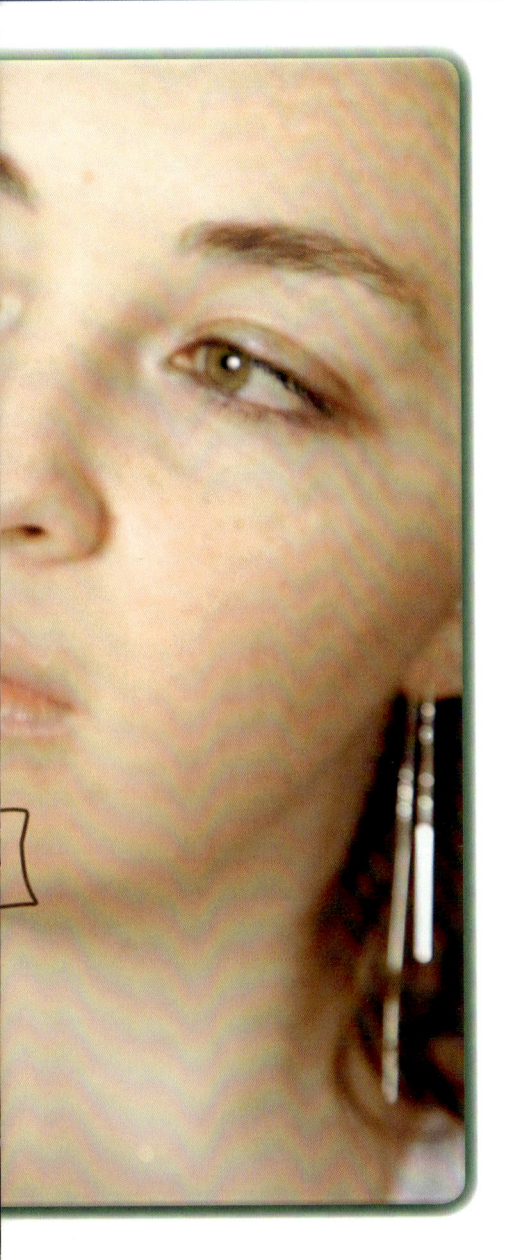

be organized in the computer's database.

To maximize the efficiency of the database, the database designer must answer some questions throughout the development of the model. Most importantly, he or she must answer the question, "What function will the database serve?" The best way to answer this question is to listen carefully to the needs of the clients or database users, clarifying their needs and extracting the key information. Here, excellent communication skills are an advantage.

The next question the database designer should ask is, "What applications [software programs] will be used to access and update information within the database?" Because different applications may access and change the database in different ways, the answer to this question affects the design of the database. For example, if multiple applications are being used and data is shared

SOFTWARE SYSTEMS FOR RUNNING DATABASES

A database designer may design a database using a software system that is already in place. Or, it may be part of the designer's job to determine what application will best support the database. Based on cost considerations and user needs, the designer typically chooses one of the following types of database management systems:

- **Desktop.** This software is meant for use with personal computers. The databases are fairly simple in design and may organize the user's personal or business information. The information is accessed from a single computer. Microsoft Access is an example of a desktop application.

- **Server.** A more costly alternative to desktop programs, server applications allow a database to be accessed through the Internet by way of a central computer. These systems can efficiently handle large amounts of information, which will be accessed by multiple users. Oracle and MySQL are common server-based systems.

- **Web-enabled.** Using this kind of software, many people can access the database from a remote location using a mobile device.

between applications, any changes to the data should appear in both programs so that the information remains accurate. If the database model does not take this into account, the integrity of the data will be lost and the database will become ineffective.

Another important question is, "What are the cost requirements of building the database?" It does not matter how great the database model is if the project of building the database is unaffordable or if maintenance of the database is too expensive. The most advanced database systems may not necessarily be the most cost-effective; implementing them could be overkill for smaller businesses or organizations.

Once these questions and others are answered, the database designer can determine the best way to organize the data. The initial data model simply shows a series of tables, or blocks of information, in a diagram. The diagram conveys the basic structure of the database and shows the connection between related tables. At this point, any changes to the information or its organization may be analyzed. The designer then creates a more detailed model. This model translates the data into SQL and assigns functions to the database management system. These functions may include how the software will maintain the data or provide security, if necessary.

DIFFERENT TYPES OF DATABASE MODELS

There are different data models that have evolved over time, through trial and error. An early, simple way to store data was a flat file system. In this system, data was simply placed into one file. It was quickly discovered that this format made accessing information a challenge, as the search had to be very specific to the data. Also, if the user searched in the wrong file, the data would never be uncovered.

Later, network and hierarchical database models were created as a way to make the data more accessible. However, these models required users to perform root searches. In a root search, the user must begin with the most basic, broad search terms, rather than entering more detailed information. For example, let's say a user is searching for a certain car part. A root search would require the user to first enter the model and make of the car in order to pull up the information. The user could not simply query the database for the car part directly. These database models are quickly becoming obsolete, as more relevant answers to the problem of how to store information are becoming clear.

In addition, the object-oriented database has come into use to store complex data, such as photos and videos. In this kind of database, information is stored as objects (numbers and code), rather than as flat data.

The development of the relational database model changed the field of database design. Today, the relational database is the most commonly used database model. Invented by Edgar F. Codd and enhanced by others in the field, the relational model allows the user to start the search from many places in the database structure, rather than starting from root terms and working up to the desired information. This model also allows multiple pieces of information to be retrieved at once. In this model, data is normalized, meaning that duplicate information is eliminated. By cutting back on multiple entries of the same information, the integrity of the system is more easily maintained. Also, required maintenance to the system is reduced. The relational database is, for now, the most advanced form of information storage.

Once a data model is chosen and created, the database designer uses SQL to input the data into the software system. In a good design, the user can continue to make additions and other changes to the data as needed without slowing down the system. While some designers deal mainly with the initial design of the system, others find that their job descriptions include making changes and continuing to manage the database.

CHAPTER 4
Managing Storage and Maintenance

The database is up and running. So the database designer's work is done, right? Not necessarily. The database designer's job usually does not end here. Since no one is more familiar with the database than the person who designed it, most companies keep the designer on to make changes as needed, or at least call on the designer occasionally to make necessary repairs to the database.

In addition to creating and implementing the initial design, other responsibilities of the database designer may include managing growth and change in the database, performance tuning, troubleshooting, modifying existing databases, backup and recovery, and instructing others in database use. Depending on the scope of the project, each of these duties could be a separate position in and of itself and fall to a different member of the IT team. However, in the case of a small company, one person is the whole IT team. This person follows every aspect of the database, from design to management and maintenance.

MANAGING GROWTH AND CHANGE

Modifications are often necessary as the needs of the users and requirements of the database management system change.

Changes in data occur on a regular basis, and a well-designed database is able to support these changes. The database designer takes future changes into account in the design and development of a data model. For example, the database designer may anticipate changes in product inventory information. Similarly, the database designer can expect that as new employees are hired within a company, the employee data will change.

Business growth also has an impact on the information within the database. Many databases are used to keep track of a business's customer history, including orders. If orders increase in volume, the database should be able to keep up with that increase. The database designer must also consider that modifications can have a domino effect. For example, major changes in the quantity of data can cause disruptions in other areas of the database.

Again, these changes are anticipated as much as possible in the initial design of the database so that preventative measures can be taken. Also, when the database designer updates information within the system, he or she makes sure that it incorporates smoothly so as to maintain data integrity. If the system has difficulty accommodating the new data, restructuring the information may become a costly endeavor. It can even result in the need for an entirely new database design.

Effectively managing change in a database is very important. A database management system that is not able to evolve along with a business will undermine the success of the business. A database that needs to be shut down frequently for repairs is not useful. If change and the possible side effects of change are anticipated, or at least caught quickly, the

Once the initial design is complete, the designer may continue to play a part in managing the database, ensuring the stability of the system.

database designer can minimize downtime. In turn, problems with the database will be less likely to hinder the growth of the business.

As well as responding to changes and seeing how they impact the database, the database designer may be responsible for making additions to the database. After all, no one is better suited to do the work of incorporating new data into the initial design. Additions and modifications to the data may be made at the level of the design. In other words, the database designer may restructure the tables that were input into the software. To do this, the database designer once again relies on SQL to recode the database and program its responses to new queries. The designer documents all of the changes that are made.

In some instances, a database designer may manage a database that he or she did not design. To do this effectively, the database professional relies on any documentation from the initial development of the database. This information is helpful in gaining an understanding of the data and how it is organized. The professional also uses the database to get a feeling for how it works. Modifications to the data are made and, if necessary, the software is upgraded.

Many database designers work solely in the area of systems upgrading. Systems may be upgraded as new technologies emerge and new software becomes available. Other database designers focus on troubleshooting. Thorough troubleshooting often leads the database designer to make modifications to an existing database. Sometimes a complete restructuring of the database management system is needed.

PERFORMANCE TUNING

Performance tuning means keeping the database running efficiently and increasing the performance of the system. Tuning is a big part of the database designer's job. A well-tuned database ensures that data can be accessed in a timely manner. It also makes the best use of computer hardware, improving the cost-effectiveness of the database. Tuning may take place at a number of different stages, beginning with the design of the database. The process can include altering the size of database files, query tuning, modifying SQL, and doing normalization (eliminating data that is duplicate). Like any well-tuned machine, the well-tuned database saves the user or business time and money. Professionals specializing in the area of performance tuning are in demand.

TROUBLESHOOTING

Whereas performance tuning is used as a preventative measure, troubleshooting takes place when a problem has already come up and needs to be resolved. Through troubleshooting, the database designer finds the source of a malfunction by going over the database management system piece by piece. The design structure is also revisited to determine if the problem occurred at the level of design. Once again, the database designer's documentation can prove extremely useful, helping him or her determine the cause of the problem.

Needless to say, troubleshooting can involve a great deal of time. While the database designer is troubleshooting, the database is down. Database downtime, as well as the cost of repairs, can add up to be a great expense. Under such circumstances, the database designer may need to work long hours in order to get the database running again. Troubleshooting is something that most database designers and business owners prefer to avoid, hence the demand for troubleshooters.

DATABASE SECURITY

Unfortunately, there are instances when problems are not resolved before data has been lost. To prevent data loss, database designers use backup systems and data recovery tools.

A TROUBLESHOOTING SCENARIO

A database malfunctions, risking the success of the business that relies on the stability of the system. What is a database designer to do? First, he or she must gather all of the information in detail from the moment the problem began. Then, he or she refers to the documentation and other records that were kept during the design process. Finally, the database designer goes step-by-step over the elements of the design to see where the failure occurred and how to make repairs.

However, preventative measures are the best action. Given the amount of valuable data that could be lost without doing anything to protect it, data backup and recovery is an essential part of the database management system. Sometimes a complete secondary system, identical to the original database management system, is created. This system can be relied upon should the original system fail or be damaged in some way.

Common causes of data loss are hardware failure, natural disasters such as storms, and user error. In each of these situations, data loss can be reduced with a good action plan. Recovery tools, installed prior to data loss, can restore the system to a point in time before the damage was done. The risk is that the system will lose changes that may have been made in the interim. A backup system is another good precautionary measure, as long as the system is backed up regularly. If the backup system is run consistently, all changes to the data are covered.

Data may also be lost due to a computer virus or other intentional attack. Again, a backup and recovery system can be helpful, but security measures can keep people from hacking into a database. Such measures often entail installing security systems. For example, the database designer can set up a system of authorization codes that allows only certain users to view certain data. Security is particularly important when the data is of a confidential nature, such as financial information. For this reason, banks and other financial institutions rely heavily on security measures.

Database designers may specialize in database security, evaluating security risks and developing security measures.

INSTRUCTING USERS IN DATABASE KNOW-HOW

Database designers spend a great deal of time educating others on how to use the database. This involves both written and verbal communication. Instruction may be limited to explaining the basic functionality of the database, including how to pose a query that will bring up the desired information. However, if the primary user is not the database designer, instruction may also include the management and maintenance of the database.

The area of IT in which the primary focus is helping users is known as the help desk. From this platform, database designers give users support by answering specific questions about the database. This may be done via software, the Internet, e-mail, or a call center. At the help desk, the database designer's communication skills become an important asset. The professional will often instruct those who have little to no computer knowledge. The complex ideas of database design and computer language must be broken down for the everyday user.

Whether working on the management of database systems, database maintenance, or user assistance, the field of database design has many areas in which one can focus. Education and training offers one the opportunity to gain knowledge about these different areas and perhaps choose an area of specialization.

CHAPTER 5
Avenues for Entering the Field

So how does one learn the tools and techniques of database design, taking steps toward the future? Begin in the here and now. There are many different classes and other learning opportunities available to aspiring database designers. Building a strong foundation in computer skills is the first step and is key to a successful career.

GETTING A HEAD START: COMPUTER LEARNING IN SECONDARY EDUCATION

Begin by getting an understanding of the general workings of a computer in high school. Most high schools offer classes in basic computing or technical education. Taking computer courses early on can help one decide what direction to take within the computer science field. Take full advantage of these courses in high school; it can save time later on, enabling one to move into higher-level courses. Courses are also available to high school students through the local department of parks and recreation or the public library.

Consider the math courses available at the high school level, and get ahead by taking classes such as algebra, pre-calculus, and calculus. Some of these math credits may be applied at the college level. Any degree related to the use of computers requires a large number of math credits. Classes in

A strong foundation in computer basics begins by taking courses at the high school level.

physics, chemistry, public speaking, English, and writing will prove valuable as well. Such classes provide a good foundation for the analytic and communication skills that are used in the field of database design.

Vocational and technical schools offer an alternative to the standard high school education. These schools focus on specific technical skills. They also provide opportunities for apprenticeships, allowing students to begin a real-world exploration of their area of interest. Like a standard high school, a vocational school offers core subjects such as English and history, but it enables students to apply these studies to their chosen career paths.

Beyond the realm of formal education, there are numerous ways to explore a general interest in computer science and a specific interest in database design. Consider joining an online or local information technology club, or perhaps starting one. Thanks to Internet resources, it is easy to reach out to others in the online community with similar interests. Even at this stage, try to stay informed about the latest advancements in the field of database design. Subscribing to computer science publications and online newsletters is a great way of staying abreast of new technology.

Once there is a general understanding of database design, get hands-on experience by trying to create a database. Learn

Aspiring database designers can learn from the experience of teachers and those working in the computer field. Trying to create a database of your own is excellent practice for the future.

by doing. Get started by organizing some of the information that is encountered in daily life. Fred Leskowitz recommends sticking with information that you know. He says, "Get started building a database to track your pet's health, to track your mom's pantry and shopping lists, to monitor your exercise. Some of the most fun can be had in seeing how data normalization theory really applies to real-world problems."

Once out of high school, there are numerous routes that may be taken to enter the field of database design. Perhaps the most direct route is earning a college degree.

POSTSECONDARY DEGREES

There are a variety of degree programs at the postsecondary (college) level that prepare students for a career in database design. One's choice will impact the time one spends pursuing a postsecondary education, as well as one's eligibility for specific positions in the workforce. Affordability is also a consideration when choosing a degree and a school. The choice of a technical institute, college, or university depends on one's intended career path. The plethora of online schools now available has added yet another element to the decision-making process. There are many reputable schools from which to choose and many degree programs to choose from as well.

An associate's degree or diploma program can take up to two years to complete. The credits earned can often be counted toward a bachelor's degree. (In most cases, a junior college or community college degree can later be applied to a higher degree.) A bachelor's degree is usually earned after the completion of a four-year program in which core education courses are required. In addition, focus is placed on a specific area of interest through one's major. Many database designers choose this route, opting for a bachelor's degree program specifically in database design or database administration. Others pursue a program under the broader umbrellas of computer science, engineering, information technology, management information systems, mathematics, or even business administration.

Either an associate's degree or a bachelor's degree will serve as a good springboard from which to enter the workforce. However, going a step further to earn a master's degree can be desirable to some employers and to those looking for

Technical schools, such as North Technical High School in Missouri, offer plenty of hands-on experience working with database management systems.

higher-level positions. Master's degrees generally take up to two additional years to earn following a four-year bachelor's program. An appropriate degree may fall under a number of headings, including master's in database administration, master's in database marketing, and master's in computer science.

One's level of education often reflects what positions may be pursued. For example, if one has no intention of being in a management position, an associate's degree or a bachelor's degree should suffice. If there is a specific area in which one would like to work within the field of database design, such as performance tuning or security, one can opt for a bachelor's degree with a concentration in the area of interest. If one does indeed wish to pursue a management position, one can start a master's program right after getting a bachelor's degree or after gaining some experience in the field.

A SAMPLING OF CLASSES

In the first year of a postsecondary, or college-level, education, most students are required to take introductory courses, unless they have taken classes in high school that allow them to skip ahead. At this level, most courses involve lectures as well as lab work. During lab periods, students work with computers, getting hands-on experience with the material. Classes required for degree programs vary, but the following are common course offerings:

- **Basic programming.** This introductory course provides information on software development and gives one a foundation in simple data structures. The roots are also set for learning documentation practices, as most courses require documentation as part of the lab requirements.

- **Introduction to computer science.** In this course, one learns the basics of how computers work and beginning problem-solving strategies. Course work may include learning to program a computer.

- **Database design and implementation.** Students learn to analyze data, organize it, and develop searches. Course work includes applying a basic design structure to information.

- **Introduction to the World Wide Web.** In this course, students usually learn how to develop a database-driven Web site using HTML, JavaScript, and other Web-based programs.

- **Computer networking.** Networking is the means by which computers communicate and share information. Through this course, students become familiar with that process. Knowledge of network operations is valuable in the database design industry. Through links to different databases, much networking occurs.

- **Technical writing.** This writing course gives students an understanding of what is needed to put the details of database design on paper. Due to the amount of documentation and written communication in this field, this course is a requirement for most degrees.

- **Calculus/discrete math.** Through these math courses, students of database design learn to apply problem-solving models to real-life situations. Learning math is important in the computer sciences, as students gain an understanding of mathematical analysis, logic, and function.

The following course listings pertain to relational database models. This type of data model has become so commonly used that degree programs have made these classes a requirement for students. Courses in this area include:

- **Relational database design.** Students taking a relational database design course gain an understanding of the terms and concepts associated with relational databases. Course requirements include creating a database table, a data structure used in relational database design, using SQL.

- **Data normalization.** In this course, students learn how to remove duplicate data from a data management system in a way that maintains the integrity of the data and increases the speed of the entire system.

- **SQL.** This course teaches SQL, one of the many programming languages with which students of database design must be familiar.

SOFTWARE CERTIFICATION PROGRAMS

Certifications in specific systems are available through a number of software companies. Look into programs such as Oracle's Certified Professional and the Microsoft Certified Database Administrator (MCDA) program. Some software-specific certification programs require students to have had some experience in the field. These programs provide working professionals with resources for continued education. Program costs may even be covered by an employer.

PROFESSIONAL CERTIFICATIONS

Another option is to earn database design certifications in place of, or in addition to, a degree. Some technical institutions, colleges, and universities have certificate programs. These programs can take up to one year to complete and include coursework and exams.

Many database designers continue their education once they are working in the field. Some designers pursue certifications in specific systems, which are available through software companies. Taking advantage of companies' independent training programs demonstrates knowledge of specific systems and can help one be more competitive in the field. However, it may not be a requirement for employment. According to Fred Leskowitz, "To get started in the field and to show potential employers that you are serious about your interest, I would definitely recommend certifications. Having on-the-job experience is important, but classes and training can save lots of time and provide better results."

When making decisions about education and training, consider what the outcome may be for each educational path. Picturing oneself in the work environment can be very helpful in the decision-making process. Database designers have many options when considering job locations, environments, and industries in which to work. A good education only increases those options.

CHAPTER 6
An Array of Opportunities

Opportunities are plentiful in the field of database design. The possibilities for employment are limitless, as virtually every organization imaginable has information that needs to be organized and managed. Database designers can be found working in small businesses, hospitals, law enforcement agencies, government offices, financial institutions, universities, computer systems companies, insurance offices, libraries, and large corporations. The possibilities are as diverse as the kinds of information that can be stored in a database.

Once the words "You're hired!" are heard, what might work life be like for a database designer?

WORK ENVIRONMENT

As a database designer, one can expect to spend most of the time working in an office space or in a computer lab in front of a computer. The majority of a database designer's work is completed at a desk.

As with many computer-related fields, there may be the risk of eyestrain, headaches, back problems from sitting for extended periods of time, and carpal tunnel syndrome from excessive typing. When considering a place of employment, it is a good idea to observe the work setting to see whether or not the employer has taken steps to protect employees' health. For example, is the lighting sufficient, and is it positioned in a way to reduce glare from the computer screen? Is there ample space to work? Are items provided to increase employees' comfort level and efficiency? If not, are employees able to bring their own comfort items to work, such as chairs or wrist rests? How many breaks are employees permitted in order to walk around and stretch? These considerations will help ensure a positive work experience.

Although this is a desk job, there is interaction with others. Examples include meeting with clients to establish needs for the database, teaching people how to use the database, and working as a member of an information technology team. Face-to-face meetings may be held at the workplace or may require traveling to client locations. Travel is generally minimal. However, it is a reality for the database designer who must go to various locations to work with different systems or consult with companies.

A benefit in this field is that many positions allow for telecommuting if an employer is receptive to it. This can sometimes give the database designer the flexibility to set his or her own work hours. The database designer's workweek is an average of forty hours, but it can be more if his or her responsibilities include troubleshooting and maintenance. Career professionals who specialize in these areas may be required to have on-call hours or work overtime in order to get a malfunctioning system running smoothly once again.

SELF-EMPLOYED OR INDEPENDENT CONTRACTOR

The profession of database designer offers many employment options. Being an employee of an organization offers stability,

A database designer who is a self-employed professional or an independent contractor will find that multitasking comes with the territory.

but some in this field choose to open their own businesses or become independent contractors. Many database designers have created successful companies that design databases or create database-driven Web sites for other businesses. Self-employment can be very rewarding, and it enables the database designer to choose clients and projects. However, it also requires the database designer to be a self-starter with business savvy and know-how.

Many of the same qualities that make one a good database designer are also fundamental for a person who is self-employed. Time management skills, attention to detail, and strong problem-solving abilities all benefit a business owner. Compared to an organizational employee, the self-employed professional has more control over his or her work environment and may enjoy a more flexible work schedule. On the other hand, some aspects of the career may be much more challenging. Employees of an organization usually have details like health care, retirement savings, and taxes largely taken care of by their employers. However, self-employed professionals must make provisions for themselves. Also, business owners spend much of their time dealing with the financial and operational aspects of their businesses, rather than focusing solely on database design.

Independent contractors or freelancers usually have clients from a variety of businesses. They are hired to complete specific projects or tasks for companies, but they are not permanent employees. They do not receive employee benefits, and taxes are not withheld. As an independent contractor, one has the freedom to choose which projects he or she would like and set his or her own work schedule. Like business owners, independent contractors must have a strong work ethic in order to meet clients' needs and deadlines.

INTERNET OPPORTUNITIES

The use of the World Wide Web has added yet another area for database design professionals to explore. Database designers and Web page developers often cooperate to create and maintain certain kinds of Web sites.

To understand how the database designer plays a role in the functionality of the World Wide Web, one must have a basic understanding of the different kinds of Web pages that exist. There are both static and dynamic Web pages. A static

PROS AND CONS OF A CAREER IN DATABASE DESIGN

All career fields have positive and negative aspects to consider. The key is to choose a career with positive aspects that you value and negative aspects that you can at least tolerate. For the field of database design, some of the pros and cons are as follows:

Pros:
- Career diversity gives database designers many options in choosing a work setting and for specializing within the field.
- Database designers have the satisfaction of seeing their designs serve a purpose.
- There is opportunity for self-employment.
- This profession offers job security and growth potential.
- Database designers may have the option of working at the job site or from home.

Cons:
- Database designers are under pressure to create a design that can withstand the test of time.
- Deadlines are often tight.
- The database design may not always reflect what is most logical or elegant, but what is the most cost-efficient for the client.
- There is the possibility of being on call and working odd hours.
- Technology changes so rapidly that what worked yesterday may not work tomorrow.

Web page looks the same and contains the same information each time it is loaded. In order for the page to change, someone must program it differently and then upload the new version. In contrast, a dynamic Web page can change each time the page is loaded. Sometimes users can even manipulate the information on the page and make changes themselves.

A database-backed, or database-driven, Web site is a type of dynamic Web page. These Web sites are connected to a database in a way that allows information to be pulled directly from the database. As the information within the database changes, the Web site reflects those changes. With proper database design, these changes are automatic, without any manipulation from the user. An example is an e-commerce site that must provide up-to-the-minute information about products and prices to customers.

As members of an IT team, database designers and Web page developers often share work on database-backed Web sites. The database designer works closely with Web developers to ensure ease of access to the data through proper coding. Many database designers who work for smaller companies or who are self-employed take on the dual role of designer and Web page developer.

As the cost of these sites has gone down and the process has become easier to manage, more businesses have been relying on database designers to help create database-backed Web sites. Database designers find their expertise and services in great demand as new technologies are released, allowing databases to be accessed from remote locations. The challenge for these database designers is in building a site that can keep up with data changes and provide the necessary security measures. The satisfaction comes from working on a database design that makes information accessible to everyone connected to the World Wide Web.

FINDING THE RIGHT JOB

With so many options, how does someone entering this field find a job that is a good fit? While receiving education and training, one should note the aspects of database design and the areas of study that he or she finds the most rewarding. In addition, one should reflect on his or her natural strengths, weaknesses, and preferences. For example, someone who has excellent communication skills and enjoys working with others may be a perfect fit for a help desk job. Those who like staying abreast of the latest technology might enjoy working with computer engineers to design new products incorporating databases. If problem solving gives one great satisfaction, performance tuning or troubleshooting may be a good niche. Those who strictly enjoy doing design work and organizing information may seek a job in which the initial design process constitutes the main workload.

As Fred Leskowitz discovered by combining his interest in library science with his interest in database design, a personal interest, or even a hobby, can sometimes lead to work in an industry that is enjoyable and rewarding. Those entering this field would benefit from examining their own interests and thinking creatively about how database design relates to those interests. For example, a sports enthusiast may want to work on databases that house sports statistics.

An internship offers the perfect opportunity for exploring a job before officially becoming an employee. An intern is a person in training who holds a temporary position in an organization. Sometimes an intern is paid, but often he or she completes the work as a volunteer. Through an internship, one can learn some of the tricks of the trade and perform tasks that will be required as a database designer. This valuable work experience can then be included on one's résumé and discussed in job interviews. An internship also offers one the chance to make connections that may lead to employment. By completing internships in more than one organization, or by observing the different roles in the same organization, one can get a bird's-eye view of what it is like to work in different areas of database design.

When starting one's journey to becoming a database designer, it is important to keep records of one's experiences and design work. Work samples may later be included in one's résumé or portfolio. This information can be used to help one get a job or home in on the job that may be the best fit.

CHAPTER 7
The Evolution of a Database Designer

As technology continues to morph, so does the job of housing vast amounts of information within the new technological systems. As a result, a professional database design must evolve in order to stay current.

STAYING ABREAST OF NEW IDEAS AND TECHNOLOGY

Even the most experienced database designer needs to stay informed about the changes in technology. In particular, one must become familiar with the newest applications and programs. New software programs can change the way databases are designed or make a database easier to manage. If a database designer stays on the cutting edge of new technology, his or her designs will be current as well.

Learning about progress in the field of database design can be done in much the same way as someone just starting out: by reading computer science publications, joining information technology groups in the community or online, and by pursuing continuing education. Joining technology organizations, for example, gives one the opportunity to network and share information with others in the same field.

Perhaps one of the most common ways to acquire new knowledge in the field is to continue taking classes in subjects

THE EVOLUTION OF A DATABASE DESIGNER | 61

By taking courses, joining technology organizations, and maintaining connections to others in the IT field, one can learn about innovations in database design.

related to database design. Continuing education may involve completing a higher degree, such as a master's degree, or it may be as simple as taking a certification course to learn a new application. As mentioned in chapter 5, such certification courses may be offered through employers, computer science organizations, or computer science companies that create the new technologies. They may also be available at a college or university, with classes held either in person or online. Lifelong learning is beneficial in any field, but in the ever-changing field of computers, it is a must for career advancement.

CAREER ADVANCEMENT

Database design is a dynamic profession. Those who choose this career can expect a variety of choices in employment and areas of specialization. With a strong educational background, experience, and management skills, a database designer is well on the path to advancing in this field.

High-level positions include that of chief technology officer, senior database administrator, lead database designer, and manager of information systems. As the titles imply, these positions require one to serve as the leader of computer science professionals or of an IT team. People in these positions oversee the design, management, and maintenance of databases. To do so, they must understand all of the tasks that accompany the process. These leaders serve as a resource for the team, while tending to the other responsibilities that come with a supervisory position. These responsibilities might include recommending the best technologies to apply to the project, making sure that the team works well together, delegating duties to IT team members, and documenting the design process of the team.

Opportunities for advancement in the workplace depend greatly on the size of the organization for which one works. Larger businesses may have multiple database designers leading different teams, while small businesses may not have someone in a management position. All aspects of the design process and duties related to systems upkeep may fall to a general database designer. For those willing to pursue the training and experience to earn high-level positions within a company, the responsibilities are great, but the benefits include higher salaries and greater job security.

Another opportunity in this field is in teaching up-and-coming database designers. One can work as a trainer in a certification program at a computer science company or as a teacher or professor at a college or university. This career path offers a different take on the profession and lends itself to more social interaction and less desk time. Also, people who train up-and-coming designers are required to stay current with the newest advances in order to pass that knowledge on to those entering the field. Whatever path is chosen, a career in database design offers those in the field ample opportunity to grow in their areas of expertise.

ADVICE FROM A PROFESSIONAL

Dean Maurice is a technical manager. As such, he oversees a team of database designers and other computer science

TOOLS FOR ADVANCEMENT

Advancement in the field of database design requires a combination of hard work, learning, and personal traits that establish one as a good leader. The following are some important characteristics and behaviors that will help one succeed in this field:

- **Positive attitude.** A positive outlook and patience go a long way in showing employers that one can work well with others and provide guidance.

- **Thirst for knowledge.** An interest in continued learning, even once in the field, means the database designer will stay informed of the newest technologies.

- **Willingness to hone special skills.** A professional can make himself or herself more valuable by finding a niche, such as tuning or security, and learning all there is to know about it.

- **Establishing and maintaining a good reputation.** Someone who is known for being reliable and respectful is likely to be taken seriously when seeking a promotion.

- **Volunteering to take on more responsibilities.** By taking on more tasks, an employee establishes his or her value within the workplace. Most employers reward an employee who is willing to step up and do the work.

professionals. To get where he is today, he has had a hand in many different aspects of information technology.

Maurice explains, "I had created DB [database] design layout for combined content retrieval for military operations—data, imagery, text multiple-source information, and formats. More recently, for the past ten years I have been part of performance testing, architectural, and design reviews, as well as having various DBAs [database administrators] and DB developers working for me or with me supporting DB design projects."

In his experience, ongoing training is a necessity, not just an opportunity. "Certification and ongoing training is

Intel Corporation's chief technology officer Justin R. Rattner speaks at a forum. Such events give professionals the opportunity to keep up with advances in the computer field.

required for everyone, no matter what your degree level," explains Maurice.

He also notes that experience and education go hand-in-hand when moving into higher-level positions. "Many times a master's would be preferred to move into management (MBA or others), but in most cases you would need experience working in the field directly to manage," he says.

The field of database design has many niches in which to gain experience. Maurice says that the diversity of this field is part of what makes it interesting. He says, "Database design is a wide-open field with many aspects, multiple disciplines, and various products and tool sets."

ON THE HORIZON

The future looks bright for those entering database design and related fields. As long as the world is on a continuous search for information, database designers will be in demand. New technologies such as mobile devices, which allow larger amounts of information to be accessed on the go, only add to the need for professionals with the know-how to organize and maintain information systems.

According to the U.S. Department of Labor, this profession is in a major growth period, which is predicted to continue well into the future. The field of database administration alone is predicted to grow by 37 percent in the period from 2006 to 2016.

In this field in which professionals are in high demand, there is good job security and income potential is better than average. Income can vary depending on one's skill level, area

THE EVOLUTION OF A DATABASE DESIGNER | 67

Chief Technology Officer Padmasree Warrior of Cisco Systems attends the kickoff of Bangalore IT.biz in 2009. The yearly conference benefits the IT industry by creating a global network of professionals.

of specialization, education level, and the complexity of the system with which one works. The most up-to-date information regarding salaries can be found at the Web site of the U.S. Bureau of Labor Statistics, http://www.bls.gov.

Initially, the job of a database designer sounds simple: organize information. However, when one considers the quantity of information, the number of people using it, and the rapidly changing technology, the vast scope of this job comes into view. Millions of people, every second of every day, rely on the work of database designers to put the world of information into order.

Glossary

application Computer software that helps the user perform a particular task.

computer platform The underlying operating system, or hardware, on which computer applications run.

data Information input into a database.

database A computer storehouse of related information.

database management system (DBMS) A collection of computer applications that allows the user to organize and manage the information within a database.

database model A diagram showing the organization and relationships among the data within a database.

data entry The act of putting information into the database, which is typically done by typing information into an entry form.

flat file A database in its most basic form, with a single table of information.

help desk A support service in which computer users can get assistance from a computer professional.

information technology (IT) team A group of professionals working together to build, store, and manage data hardware and software systems.

interface The place where the user can see and interact with the data contained in the database, generally on a screen.

niche A special area of demand for a product or service.

normalization The process of removing duplicate entries from a database.

performance tuning The process of ensuring that a computer system, such as a database, is working at a level of maximum efficiency.

query A question posed to a database in order to extract information.

relation A logical association between two or more things.

relational database A type of database structure that allows the user to access information from anywhere within the structure.

structured query language (SQL) A computer programming language used to access and manipulate data in a relational database.

systematize To put in order.

troubleshooting The act of methodically searching for the source of a computer system malfunction.

For More Information

Association for Computing Machinery (ACM)
2 Penn Plaza, Suite 701
New York, NY 10121
(800) 342-6626
Web site: http://www.acm.org
Along with serving as a career resource, the ACM has a publication called *Crossroads* that is written for students by students.

Association of Information Technology Professionals (AITP)
401 North Michigan Avenue, Suite 2400
Chicago, IL 60611
(800) 224-9371
Web site: http://www.aitp.org
AITP members have the opportunity to network and make connections with others in the IT field.

Canadian Information Processing Society (CIPS)
5090 Explorer Drive, Suite 801
Mississauga, ON L4W 4T9
Canada
(877) 275-2477
Web site: http://www.cips.ca
This organization sets standards in the information technology field and supports professionals on issues affecting the industry.

Computer Science Teachers Association (CSTA)
P.O. Box 30778

New York, NY 10117
(800) 342-6626
Web site: http://www.csta.acm.org
Serving as a resource for teachers as well as students, the CSTA aims to increase the availability of computer science programs in schools and improve computer science curricula.

IEEE Computer Society
2001 L Street NW, Suite 700
Washington, DC 20036-4910
(800) 272-6657
Web site: http://www.computer.org
This organization offers a wide range of career-building resources for computer science professionals, including certifications and publications.

Information Technology Alliance (ITA)
23940 North 73rd Place
Scottsdale, AZ 85255
(480) 515-2003
Web site: http://www.italliance.com
The ITA is a networking organization, with members exchanging ideas and the latest information about the field of information technology.

Information Technology Industry Council (ITI)
1101 K Street NW, Suite 610
Washington, DC 20005
(202) 737-8888

Web site: http://www.itic.org
The council is an advocate for the IT community, helping members to navigate government relations and trade policies, as well as environmental issues such as electronics recycling and sustainability.

TechAmerica
1401 Wilson Boulevard, Suite 1100
Arlington, VA 22209
(703) 522-5055
Web site: http://www.itaa.org
TechAmerica sets standards in the technology sector and serves as a trade association that creates growth within the industry.

WEB SITES

Due to the changing nature of Internet links, Rosen Publishing has developed an online list of Web sites related to the subject of this book. This site is updated regularly. Please use this link to access the list:

http://www.rosenlinks.com/cict/cidd

For Further Reading

Dice Career Solutions, Inc. *The Official Dice Technology Job Search Guide.* Hoboken, NJ: Wiley, 2007.

Ferguson's Careers in Focus: Computers. New York, NY: Ferguson, 2008.

Gillenson, Mark L., et al. *Introduction to Database Management* (Wiley Pathways). Hoboken, NJ: Wiley, 2008.

Goldberg, Jan, and Mark Rowh. *Great Jobs for Computer Science Majors.* Chicago, IL: VGM Career Books, 2003.

Harrington, Jan L. *Relational Database Design and Implementation: Clearly Explained.* Boston, MA: Morgan Kaufmann/Elsevier, 2009.

Hernandez, Michael James. *Database Design for Mere Mortals: A Hands-On Guide to Relational Database Design.* Boston, MA: Addison-Wesley, 2003.

Kirk, Amanda. *Information Technology* (Field Guides to Finding a New Career). New York, NY: Ferguson, 2009.

Kroenke, David, and David J. Auer. *Database Concepts.* 4th ed. Upper Saddle River, NJ: Prentice Hall, 2010.

Moreira, Paula. *Ace the IT Résumé.* 2nd ed. New York, NY: McGraw-Hill, 2007.

Peters, Craig. *Larry Ellison: Database Genius of Oracle* (Internet Biographies). Berkeley Heights, NJ: Enslow Publishers, 2003.

Powell, Gavin. *Beginning Database Design.* Hoboken, NJ: Wiley, 2006.

Reeves, Diane Lindsey, Gail Karlitz, and Don Rauf. *Career Ideas for Teens in Information Technology.* New York, NY: Checkmark, 2006.

Rob, Peter, and Carlos Coronel. *Database Systems: Design, Implementation, and Management.* 9th ed. Australia; United States: Course Technology Cengage Learning, 2011.

Sciore, Edward. *Database Design and Implementation.* Hoboken, NJ: Wiley, 2009.

Spraul, V. Anton. *Computer Science Made Simple* (Made Simple). New York, NY: Broadway Books, 2005.

Stephens, Rod. *Beginning Database Design Solutions* (Wrox Beginning Guides). Hoboken, NJ: Wiley, 2009.

Wyckoff, Claire. *Computers and Information Technology* (Top Careers in Two Years). New York, NY: Ferguson, 2008.

Bibliography

Bureau of Labor Statistics. "Computer Network, Systems, and Database Administrators." *Occupational Outlook Handbook, 2010–11 Edition.* December 17, 2009. Retrieved January 5, 2009 (http://www.bls.gov/oco/ocos305.htm).

Bureau of Labor Statistics. "Computer Software Engineers and Computer Programmers." *Occupational Outlook Handbook, 2010–11 Edition.* December 17, 2009. Retrieved January 5, 2009 (http://www.bls.gov/oco/ocos303.htm).

Churcher, Clare. *Beginning Database Design: From Novice to Professional.* Berkeley, CA: Apress; New York, NY: Springer-Verlag, 2007.

Daniels, Charles F. "Computer Ergonomics." 1996. Retrieved March 17, 2010 (http://www.klis.com/computers+health).

Davidson, Louis. "Ten Common Database Design Mistakes." February 26, 2007. Retrieved January 20, 2010 (http://www.simple-talk.com/sql/database-administration/ten-common-database-design-mistakes).

Department of Mathematics and Computer Science. "Computer Science Course Descriptions." Hobart and William Smith Colleges. Retrieved March 18, 2010 (http://math.hws.edu/dept/cs_courses.html).

Leskowitz, Fred. E-mail interview with author, January 14, 2010.

Maurice, Dean. E-mail interview with author, December 29, 2009.

Mullins, Craig S. "Database Trends: Managing Database Change." October 2000. Retrieved January 15, 2010 (http://www.craigsmullins.com/dbt_1000.htm).

National Science Foundation. "Chapter 1: Elementary and Secondary Education—Information Technology in Schools." Science and Engineering Indicators 2004. Division of Science Resources Statistics, May 2004. Retrieved January 15, 2010 (http://www.nsf.gov/statistics/seind04/c1/c1s7.htm).

Sol, Selena. "Types of Databases." UK Web Design Company, 2010. Retrieved January 15, 2010 (http://www.theukwebdesigncompany.com/articles/types-of-databases.php).

Teorey, Toby J., Sam Lightstone, and Tom Nadeau. *Database Modeling and Design: Logical Design.* 4th ed. Amsterdam, the Netherlands: Elsevier; Boston, MA: Morgan Kaufmann Publishers, 2005.

Index

A

advancement, tools for, 64
apprenticeships, 43
authorization codes, 40

B

backup and recovery plans, 19, 21, 34, 38–40

C

carpel tunnel syndrome, 52
certification programs, 50–51, 62, 63, 65
classes, sampling of, 47–49
Codd, Edgar F., 32
computer science, 42, 44, 46, 48, 60, 62, 63
computer viruses, 40
customer profiles, 4, 35

D

database, definition of, 4, 6–7
database design
    definition of, 8–9
    entering the field of, 42–51
    introduction to, 4–12
    opportunities in, 11–12, 52–59
    organizing data and, 23–33
    pros and cons of a career in, 56
database designer
    evolution of a, 60–68
    person behind title of, 9–10, 13–22
    questions considered by a, 20
database management system (DBMS), 7, 24, 30, 35, 39
database models, 26–29, 31
database security, 10, 20, 38–40, 47
database terminology, 23–26
data entry, 24, 33
data models, 8, 18, 19, 23, 31–33
desktop programs, 30
disaster recovery, 10

E

employee records, 5

F

financial records, 6, 40
flat file systems, 32

G

government agencies, 4, 6, 52

H

help desk, 14, 41
hierarchical databases, 32
HTML, 48

I

independent contractors, 53–55
Information Age, 5

information technology (IT), 5, 6, 10, 13, 14, 17, 19, 34, 41, 46, 53, 57, 62, 63, 65
internships, 21, 58–59

J

JavaScript, 48

L

Leskowitz, Fred, 21–22, 45, 50–51, 58
libraries, 4, 22, 42, 52, 58
library science, 21, 22, 58

M

Maurice, Dean, 63, 65–66
Microsoft, 50
multitasking, 16, 17
museums, 4

N

network databases, 32

O

object-oriented databases, 32
Oracle, 50

P

performance tuning, 10, 34, 37–38, 47
portable electronic devices, 12
postsecondary degrees, 45–47
product inventories, 4
project budgets, 20, 31

Q

queries, 19, 24–26, 32, 33, 37, 49

R

relational databases, 26, 32–33, 49
research institutions, 4
root searches, 32

S

sales transactions, 6
self-employment, 10, 53–55, 56, 57
server applications, 30
software systems for running databases, 29, 30
storage and maintenance, managing, 5, 7, 24, 34–41
structured query language (SQL), 26, 31, 33, 37, 49

T

technical writing, 48–49
time management, 16, 17, 54
troubleshooting, 10, 34, 37, 38, 39, 53

U

U.S. Bureau of Labor Statistics, 68
U.S. Department of Labor, 66
user interfaces, 25–26

W

Web-enabled software, 30
World Wide Web, 11, 24, 30, 44, 48, 54, 55, 57–58, 68

ABOUT THE AUTHOR

Erin K. McGuire is a writer experienced in the area of career and educational resources. Along with *Careers in Graphic Arts and Computer Graphics*, published by Rosen Publishing, she has written articles related to information technology and computer science for *NextStep* magazine and Bridges Transitions, Inc. McGuire lives in East Hampton, Connecticut, with her sons, Rowan and Malachi.

PHOTO CREDITS

Cover (background, front and back), p. 1 (top left, background) © www.istockphoto.com/Audrey Prokhorov; cover (front inset), 14, 16, 28–29, 40 Shutterstock; p. 7 © www.istockphoto.com/Damir Spanic; chapter art © www.istockphoto.com/Daniel Brunner; pp. 9, 20, 30, 39, 50, 56, 64 (interior background) © www.istockphoto.com/Nicholas Belton; p. 11 Kimberly White/Reuters/Landov; p. 18 B. Busco/Getty Images; p. 24 © www.istockphoto.com/Ermin Gutenberger; p. 36 Riser/LWA/Getty Images; pp. 43, 44, 46, 67 © AP Images; p. 54 Marc Romanelli/The Image Bank/Getty Images; p. 61 Ryan McVay/Stone/Getty Images; p. 65 David Paul Morris/Getty Images.

Designer: Matthew Cauli; Editor: Andrea Sclarow; Photo Researcher: Marty Levick